EDGE BOOKS

RECYCLED SCIENCE

COOL
PLASTIC BOTTLE
AND MILK JUG
SCIENCE

BY TAMMY ENZ

Consultant:
Marcelle A. Siegel
Associate Professor of Science Education
University of Missouri

CAPSTONE PRESS
a capstone imprint

Edge Books are published by Capstone Press,
1710 Roe Crest Drive, North Mankato, Minnesota 56003
www.mycapstone.com

Library of Congress Cataloging-in-Publication Data
Names: Enz, Tammy, author.
Title: Cool plastic bottle and milk jug science / by Tammy Enz.
Description: North Mankato, Minnesota : Capstone Press, [2017] | Series: Edge books. Recycled
science | Includes bibliographical references and index.
Identifiers: LCCN 2015045604|
ISBN 9781515708629 (library binding) |
ISBN 9781515708667 (eBook PDF)
Subjects: LCSH: Plastic bottle craft—Juvenile literature. | Plastic bottles—Juvenile literature. |
Handicraft—Juvenile literature. | Science—Study and teaching—Juvenile literature. | Recycling
(Waste, etc.)—Juvenile literature.
Classification: LCC TT297 .E69 2017 | DDC 745.5—dc23
LC record available at http://lccn.loc.gov/2015045604

Editorial Credits
Brenda Haugen, editor; Russell Griesmer, designer; Tracy Cummins, media specialist;
Kathy McColley, production specialist

Photo Credits
Capstone Studio: Karon Dubke

Design elements provided by Shutterstock: bimka, FINDEEP, fourb, Golbay, jannoon028, mexrix,
Picsfive, Sarunyu_foto, STILLFX, Your Design

Printed and bound in the USA. .
009696F16

TABLE OF CONTENTS

COOL PLASTIC
BOTTLE SCIENCE

PLASTIC WITH PURPOSE

Milk, water, juice, pop—it seems like every drink comes in a plastic bottle. When you're done quenching your thirst, where do those bottles go? And where do they come from in the first place? Learn the answers to these questions and more. Then check out exciting ways to repurpose bottles and jugs into cool science experiments. Dig into your recycling bin, and get started.

GREAT PACIFIC GARBAGE PATCH

Plastic bottles are useful and durable. However, if not recycled they often end up in the Great Pacific Garbage Patch. Some scientists think this patch could twice the size of Texas. Ocean currents trap trash dumped on land in the waters of Asia and North America. Bottles can spend years floating in this garbage patch, breaking down into tiny pieces called microplastics. Sea animals often mistake plastic pieces for food. Eating plastic can kill them.

CLOUD IN A BOTTLE

Seeing a cloud in the sky might not seem remarkable. But there's a recipe for making clouds. Meet all the conditions, and you can whip one up in your kitchen!

BRANCH OF SCIENCE: **EARTH SCIENCE**
CONCEPT: **CLOUD FORMATION**

YOU'LL NEED:

- Clean 2-liter soda bottle with cap
- Water
- Dark sheet of construction paper
- Flashlight
- Matches
- A friend

PUT IT TOGETHER:

STEP 1: Fill the bottom of the bottle with about 1 inch (2.5 centimeters) of water. Screw on the cap. Shake the water around in the bottle.

STEP 2: Prop the paper against a wall. Set the bottle in front of it. Squeeze it tightly. Let go.

STEP 3: As you let go, have a friend shine the flashlight into the bottle. Do you see a cloud?

STEP 4: Have an adult light two matches at the same time. Uncap the bottle, and drop the matches in the water. Quickly replace the cap.

STEP 5: Shake the bottle, and set it against the paper.

STEP 6: Squeeze the bottle tightly, and let it go while a friend shines light on the bottle. For a few seconds you will see a cloud appear.

STEP 7: Repeatedly squeeze the bottle to see the cloud form again and again.

STEP 7

REUSABLE KNOWLEDGE:

By shaking the bottle, you filled it with water vapor. Squeezing the bottle increased the air pressure and the temperature. Releasing the bottle decreased the air pressure and lowered the temperature. Cooling water vapor formed droplets, which clung to the smoke inside. When these things happen in the atmosphere, clouds form. Dust, smoke, or volcanic ash in the air help out.

FAST FACT:

Bottles and many plastic packages are made from polyethylene terephthalate (PET). PET is a strong lightweight plastic. Its long chains of repeating molecules make it easy to form. Carbon dioxide can't seep through PET, making it ideal for soda bottles.

water vapor—water in its gaseous state

atmosphere—layer of gases surrounding Earth

MILK JUG SIPHON

Think you can get water to flow uphill? How about keeping it flowing to drain a jug dry? You bet. It's easy to do and fun to watch again and again with this experiment.

BRANCH OF SCIENCE: EARTH SCIENCE
CONCEPT: ATMOSPHERIC PRESSURE

YOU'LL NEED:

- 2 clean milk jugs
- Food coloring (any color)
- 8-10 feet (2.5-3 m) clean, clear plastic hose

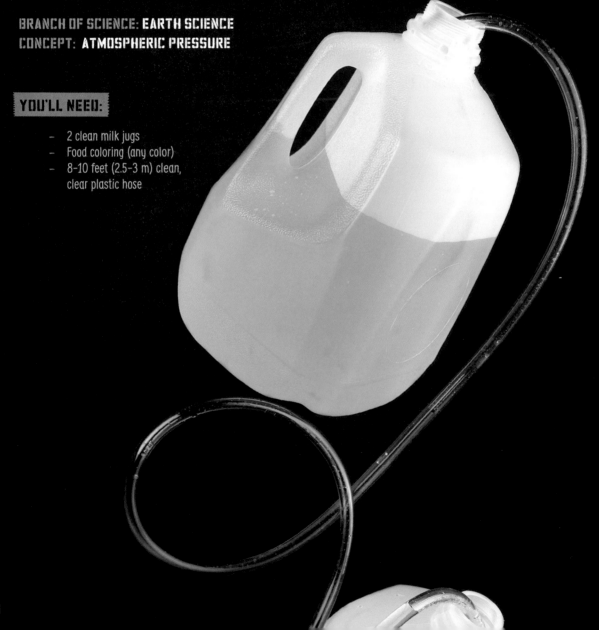

PUT IT TOGETHER:

STEP 1: Fill one jug with tap water. Add several drops of food coloring.

STEP 2: Set this jug on a table or counter.

STEP 3: Set the other jug on the floor nearby.

STEP 4: Insert the hose into the top jug. Push it all the way in. Make sure its end is near the bottom of the jug.

STEP 5: Place the other end of the hose near the bottom jug. Include some loops in the hose.

STEP 6: Gently suck on the bottom end of the hose. As the water nears your mouth, quickly stick the end inside the bottom jug. What happens?

STEP 6

REUSABLE KNOWLEDGE:

Did you realize that the air around you is constantly pushing on you? This pressure is called atmospheric pressure. It's what makes a siphon work. Sucking air out of the tube decreases the pressure inside. This causes atmospheric pressure to push water into the tube. As the water moves through the tube, its pressure is lowered again. Atmospheric pressure keeps pushing until the jug is dry.

RECYCLING MILK JUGS

Milk jugs are recycled into soap bottles, garden products, and plastic lumber. 3D printers even use old milk jugs for printing material. Why not use old milk jugs to make more milk jugs? Used jugs could contain impurities, making them unsafe for food packaging.

atmospheric pressure—pressure caused by the weight of the atmosphere

CARTESIAN DIVER

Your command of this little diver will amaze you. You can thank the properties of gases for this experiment.

BRANCH OF SCIENCE: CHEMISTRY
CONCEPT: BOYLE'S LAW

YOU'LL NEED:

- Clean empty 2-liter soda bottle with cap
- Ruler
- Water
- Small sauce packet

PUT IT TOGETHER:

STEP 1: Fill the bottle with water to within 2 inches (5 cm) of the top.

STEP 2: Drop a sauce packet into the bottle. Make sure it floats just below the water. Experiment with several packets until you find one that works.

STEP 3: Screw the cap on the bottle.

STEP 4: Squeeze the bottle. What happens?

STEP 5: Let it go. What happens now?

REUSABLE KNOWLEDGE:

An air pocket inside the packet keeps it light enough to float. When you squeeze the bottle, the air pocket becomes smaller. Now the "diver" sinks. This marvel is explained by Boyle's Law. Boyle's Law states that increasing pressure will decrease volume and vice versa.

FAST FACT:

Water is very heavy. It weighs 64 pounds per cubic foot (1,025 kilograms per cubic meter). The deeper a diver goes under water, the more pressure he feels. Deep-water divers cannot breathe because of the pressure on their lungs. Pressurized air from a SCUBA tank gives lungs enough pressure to combat water pressure. SCUBA stands for Self-Contained Underwater Breathing Apparatus.

UPSIDE DOWN WATER

Water can easily flow through a window screen, right? Not so fast! In this experiment water does the unthinkable.

BRANCH OF SCIENCE: CHEMISTRY
CONCEPT: SURFACE TENSION

YOU'LL NEED:

- Clean, empty milk jug
- Water
- 6-inch (15-cm) square of vinyl window screen
- Rubber band
- Several toothpicks
- A friend

PUT IT TOGETHER:

STEP 1: Fill the jug about 1/3 full of water.

STEP 2: Place the screen over the opening in the jug. Wrap the rubber band around the screen to hold it to the neck of the milk jug.

STEP 3: Outside or over a sink, carefully turn the jug upside down. Hold on to the jug's handle.

STEP 4: Steady the jug while holding the handle. Make sure not to squeeze it. What happens?

STEP 5: Have a friend carefully push a toothpick through a hole in the screen. What happens?

STEP 2

REUSABLE KNOWLEDGE:

Water molecules are strongly attracted to one another. This attraction is called cohesion. Under water's surface, molecules are attracted equally in all directions. This attraction is unequal at the water's surface. Here water molecules are attracted inward only. So molecules act like a thin elastic skin where they meet air. We call this surface tension. This skin stretches across the screen holes. It holds water inside the jug.

molecule—the smallest particle of a substance with the properties of that substance

cohesion—ability to stick together

surface tension—water molecules form stronger bonds at the surface, causing the surface to act like a membrane

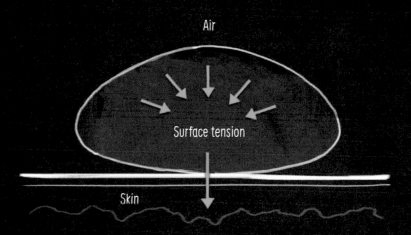

Air

Surface tension

Skin

A WATERY SKIN

Surface tension acts like a skin on water's surface. Small drops of liquid are spherical because cohesion pulls the molecules inward.

BALLOON INFLATOR

Blowing up balloons can wear out your lungs.
Let something else do the work. A little
chemical reaction is all it takes.

BRANCH OF SCIENCE: CHEMISTRY
CONCEPT: ACID/BASE REACTION

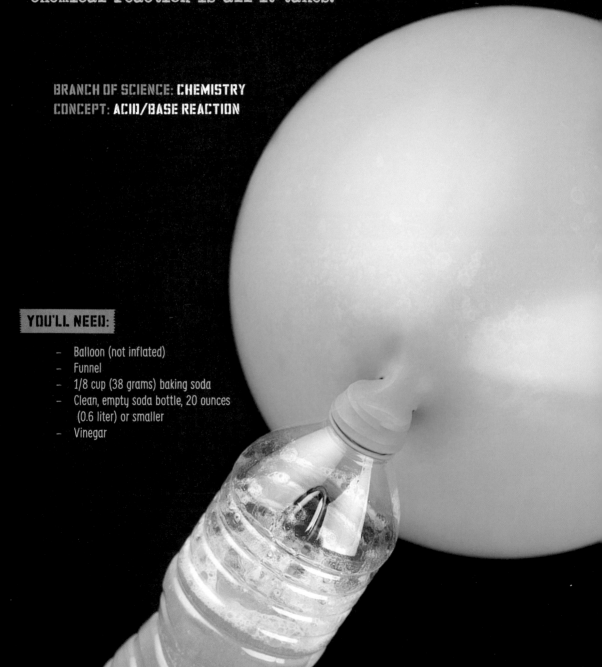

YOU'LL NEED:

- Balloon (not inflated)
- Funnel
- 1/8 cup (38 grams) baking soda
- Clean, empty soda bottle, 20 ounces
  (0.6 liter) or smaller
- Vinegar

PUT IT TOGETHER:

STEP 1: Place the tip of the funnel inside the balloon.

STEP 2: Pour the baking soda into the funnel. Shake the baking soda into the balloon.

STEP 3: Fill the bottle about half full of vinegar.

STEP 4: Remove the funnel. Stretch the neck of the balloon over the top of the bottle. Make sure none of the baking soda falls into the vinegar.

STEP 5: Hold the neck of the balloon tightly to the bottle. Tip the balloon to dump the baking soda into the vinegar. What happens?

STEP 1

STEP 4

REUSABLE KNOWLEDGE:

Vinegar is an acid, and baking soda is a base. Acids and bases react to make a new product. In this case, carbon dioxide gas is made. You can't always see a gas, but in this experiment the gas is easy to detect. It expands to fill the balloon. If you've ever made a cake, you've seen an acid and base reaction. Bubbles from reacting ingredients make the cake light and fluffy.

RECYCLING SODA BOTTLES

Think you'd look good wearing soda bottles? How about using them to decorate your home? That's exactly where most recycled PET ends up. It is processed into many new materials including carpet fiber, T-shirt fabric, shoes, and luggage. It is also used to make new PET containers for food and non-food products.

acid—sour tasting substance that reacts with a base

base—bitter tasting substance that reacts with an acid

VINEGAR ROCKET

A blasting rocket is an exciting experiment. This rocket uses things you find around your house. It packs a punch and explains an important physics law.

BRANCH OF SCIENCE: PHYSICS
CONCEPT: NEWTON'S THIRD LAW OF MOTION

PUT IT TOGETHER:

STEP 1: Fill the bottle about 1/3 full of vinegar. Set it aside.

STEP 2: Place the baking soda in the center of the toilet tissue. Carefully roll the tissue into a tight tube around the baking soda.

STEP 3: Fold the ends over, and tape them in place to make a small packet. Make sure the packet is small enough to fit inside the mouth of the pop bottle.

STEP 4: Find an open area outside. Place the cardboard canister on the ground or prop it at an angle with bricks or rocks. Make sure the canister is not pointing toward people, animals, or windows.

STEP 5: Drop the packet into the bottle. Quickly cork it. Put it cork side down inside the canister.

STEP 6: Back several yards (meters) away, and wait. It may take a little while for the rocket to take off. Do not go near it as you wait!

STEP 7: Search out the landing place of your rocket. Then do the experiment again!

STEP 2

STEP 5

REUSABLE KNOWLEDGE:

This experiment shows Newton's Third Law of Motion. This law states that for every action there is an equal and opposite reaction. The vinegar and baking soda reaction forms carbon dioxide. The carbon dioxide explodes backward from the bottle. An equal force pushes the bottle forward. This is the same principle that lifts rockets into space.

SUB IRRIGATED PLANTER

Do you like gardening? Are you sometimes afraid of watering your plants too little or too much? Try this project. It uses an important biology concept to keep plants watered just right.

BRANCH OF SCIENCE: BIOLOGY
CONCEPT: CAPILLARY ACTION

YOU'LL NEED:

- Clean, empty 2-liter bottle
- Ruler
- Marker
- Utility knife
- 3 strips of cotton from an old t-shirt, 1 inch wide x 4 inches long (2.5 cm x 10 cm)
- 3 cups (700 g) potting soil
- Lettuce or herb seeds
- Water

SAFETY FIRST:

Have an adult help when using sharp tools such as a utility knife.

STEP 1: Make a mark 3 inches (8 cm) from the top of the bottle. Use the utility knife to cut a small "x" at this spot.

STEP 2: Repeat Step 1 to make a total of six small x's. Make them evenly spaced around the bottle 3 inches (8 cm) from the top.

STEP 3: Use the utility knife to cut off the top half of the bottle.

STEP 4: Turn the top upside down, and place it inside the bottom half.

STEP 5: Lay the fabric strips inside the top part of the bottle. They should extend through the neck of the bottle and touch the bottle's bottom.

STEP 6: Pack the soil in around the cotton strips.

STEP 3

STEP 5

STEP 7: Plant seeds in the soil according to the package directions. Lightly water the seeds from the top.

STEP 8: Lift the top, and pour several inches of water into the bottle bottom. Replace the top.

STEP 9: Wait for your seeds to sprout and grow. Refill the bottom with water as needed.

REUSABLE KNOWLEDGE:

Like a straw, plant cells draw water and minerals upward. This upward flow is called capillary action. Your waterer also uses capillary action. Water moves through openings in the cotton and soil to reach the plant's roots.

capillary action—ability of liquid to flow in small places against the force of gravity

LAVA LAMP

A lava lamp gives off a one-of-a-kind glow.
Its dancing blobs bring hours of enjoyment.
Make your own with this project. Then pride
yourself on knowing the science behind it.

BRANCH OF SCIENCE: CHEMISTRY
CONCEPT: OIL AND WATER IMMISCIBILITY

YOU'LL NEED:

- Clean pop or water bottle (any size)
- Water
- Vegetable oil
- Food coloring (any color)
- Effervescent tablets (Alka-Seltzer)
- Battery-operated tea light

PUT IT TOGETHER:

STEP 1: Fill the bottle about 1/4 full of water.

STEP 2: Pour vegetable oil into the bottle until it is nearly full.

STEP 3: Drop 6 to 10 drops of food coloring into the bottle. Shake the bottle if needed to dissolve the food coloring.

STEP 4: Wait until the water and oil have separated. Place 1/4 of an effervescent tablet into the bottle. Watch the show!

STEP 5: When the bubbles stop, place another 1/4 tablet into the bottle. This time place the lit tea light upside down in the top of the bottle.

STEP 6: Take the lamp into a dark room for a lava lamp experience.

STEP 7: Add more tablets, 1/4 at a time, to keep the fun going.

STEP 4

REUSABLE KNOWLEDGE:

The oil and water don't mix together. Why? Water is much denser than oil. Its molecules are more tightly packed together than oil's are. This makes water sink. The structure of the molecules is different for oil and water too. Water's molecules are polar, meaning they have a negative charge on one end and a positive charge on the other. Their charges hold the molecules to each other. Oil is nonpolar, without a charge, and doesn't mingle with the water molecules. The fizzing tablet releases gas. As the gas rises to the surface, it pulls colored water with it. After the gas escapes, the water blobs sink back to the bottom of the bottle.

polar—molecule with one slightly positively charged and one slightly negatively charge end

nonpolar—uncharged molecule

COMPOSTING WORM FARM

Recycle more than a soda bottle with this project. Recycle your kitchen scraps too. This project does more than keep garbage out of a landfill. It improves the environment!

BRANCH OF SCIENCE: BIOLOGY
CONCEPT: SOIL SCIENCE

YOU'LL NEED:

- Clean, empty 2-liter bottle
- Utility knife
- 16.9-ounce (0.5-liter) water bottle filled with room temperature water
- Small scoop
- Ruler
- Sand
- Soil
- Fruit and vegetable peels
- 1/2 cup (0.12 liters) water
- 3 or 4 earthworms

SAFETY FIRST:

Have an adult help when using sharp tools such as a utility knife.

PUT IT TOGETHER:

STEP 1: Use the utility knife to cut the top off the 2-liter bottle. Cut it where the bottle starts to get narrower near the top. Discard the top.

STEP 2: Place the water bottle centered inside the 2-liter bottle. This will keep the worms near the outside of the bottle so you can watch them.

STEP 3: Carefully scoop about 1 inch (2.5 cm) of sand into the larger bottle. Make sure the water bottle stays in place.

STEP 4: Add about 1 inch (2.5 cm) of soil.

STEP 5: Add a layer of fruit and vegetable peels.

STEP 6: Continue layering 1-inch (2.5-cm) layers of sand, soil, and scraps. Stop when you reach about 2 inches (5 cm) from the top of the bottle.

STEP 2

STEP 5

STEP 7: Slowly pour water over the layers to make them slightly damp.

STEP 8: Add the worms.

STEP 9: Place the bottle in a cool, dark place.

STEP 10: Add small amounts of water every couple days to keep the worm farm moist. Watch daily until the worms have composted all the scraps.

STEP 11: After several weeks, pour the newly composted soil and worms into a planter or garden. Let them continue their work.

REUSABLE KNOWLEDGE:

Worms are nature's great recyclers. Worms turn food scraps and dead plants into rich soil fertilizer. As worms eat, their bodies change scraps into compost. They poop out this fertilizer to keep plants strong and healthy. Test out how well fertilizer works. Do plants grow better in composted soil or regular soil?

compost—breaks down fruits, vegetables, and other materials to make soil better for gardening

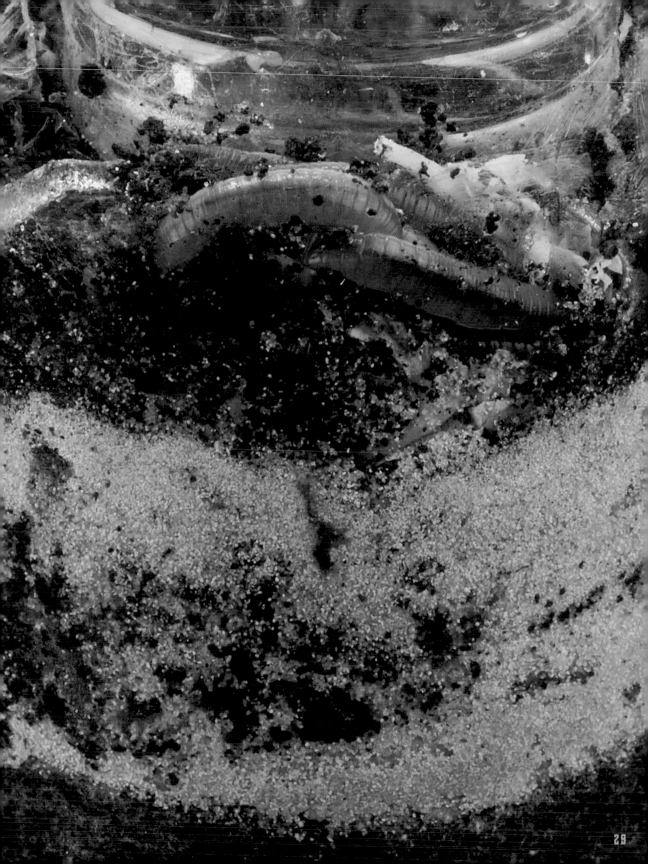

GLOSSARY

acid—sour tasting substance that reacts with a base

atmosphere—layer of gases surrounding Earth

atmospheric pressure—pressure caused by the weight of the atmosphere

base—bitter tasting substance that reacts with an acid

capillary action—ability of liquid to flow in small places against the force of gravity

cohesion—ability to stick together

compost—breaks down fruits, vegetables, and other materials to make soil better for gardening

molecule—the smallest particle of a substance with the properties of that substance

nonpolar—uncharged molecule

polar—molecule with one slightly positively charged and one slightly negatively charge end

surface tension—water molecules form stronger bonds at the surface, causing the surface to act like a membrane

water vapor—water in its gaseous state

READ MORE

Enz, Tammy. *Repurpose It: Invent New Uses for Old Stuff.* Invent It. North Mankato, Minn.: Capstone Press, 2012.

Lepetit, Angie. *Trash Magic: A Book about Recycling a Plastic Bottle.* Earth Matters. North Mankato, Minn.: Capstone Press, 2013.

Offill, Jenny. *11 Experiments that Failed.* New York: Schwartz & Wade Books, 2011.

INTERNET SITES

FactHound offers a safe, fun way to find Internet sites related to this book. All of the sites on FactHound have been researched by our staff.

Here's all you do:
Visit *www.facthound.com*
Type in this code: 9781515708629

Check out projects, games and lots more at
www.capstonekids.com

CRITICAL THINKING USING THE COMMON CORE

1. Describe the two concepts that cause bubbles to rise and drop back in the lava lamp project. (Key Ideas and Details)

2. Water is held inside an upside down jug with a window screen. What term describes water's ability to do this? (Craft and Structure)

3. Describe how a bottle dropped in a California river might make its way to the Great Pacific Garbage Patch? (Integration of Knowledge and Ideas)

INDEX